let's cook

soups

Carole
Clements

Contents

Fresh Mushroom Soup

When you see mushrooms at a special price in your local supermarket, think of this soup.
Chestnut, portobello or horse mushrooms are especially tasty.

Serves 4

INGREDIENTS

40 g/1½ oz/3 tbsp butter
700 g/1 lb 9 oz mushrooms, sliced
1 onion, finely chopped
1 shallot, finely chopped
25 g/1 oz/3 tbsp plain (all-purpose)
   flour

2–3 tbsp dry white wine or sherry
1.4 litres/2½ pints/6 cups chicken
   or vegetable stock
150 ml/5 fl oz/⅔ cup single (light)
   cream

2 tbsp chopped fresh parsley
fresh lemon juice (optional)
salt and pepper
4 tbsp soured cream or crème fraîche,
   to garnish

1 Melt half the butter in a large frying pan (skillet) over a medium heat. Add the mushrooms and season with salt and pepper. Cook for about 8 minutes until they are golden brown, stirring occasionally at first, then more often after they start to colour. Remove the mushrooms from the heat.

2 Melt the remaining butter in a saucepan over a medium heat, add the onion and shallot and cook for 2–3 minutes until just softened. Stir the flour into the pan and continue cooking for 2 minutes. Add the wine and stock and stir well.

3 Set aside about one-quarter of the mushrooms. Add the remainder to the pan. Reduce the heat, cover and cook gently for 20 minutes, stirring occasionally.

4 Allow the soup to cool slightly, then transfer to a blender or food processor and purée until smooth, working in batches, if necessary. (If using a food processor, strain off the cooking liquid and reserve. Purée the soup solids with enough cooking liquid to moisten them, then combine with the remaining liquid.)

5 Return the soup to the saucepan and stir in the reserved mushrooms, the cream and parsley. Cook for about 5 minutes to heat through. Taste and adjust the seasoning, adding a few drops of lemon juice if wished. Ladle into warm bowls and decorate with soured cream.

Fresh Tomato Soup

Made with fresh tomatoes, the taste of this soup is subtle and complex.
Basil is a proven partner for tomatoes, but you could also try tarragon.

Serves 4

INGREDIENTS

1 kg/2 lb 4 oz ripe plum tomatoes,
  skinned
2 tsp olive oil
1 large sweet onion, finely chopped
1 carrot, finely chopped

1 stalk celery, finely chopped
2 garlic cloves, finely chopped or
  crushed
1 tsp fresh marjoram leaves, or ¼ tsp
  dried marjoram

450 ml/16 fl oz/ 2 cups water
4–5 tbsp double (heavy) cream, plus
  extra to garnish
2 tbsp chopped fresh basil leaves
salt and pepper

1 Cut the tomatoes in half and scrape the seeds into a sieve set over a bowl to catch the juice. Reserve the juice and discard the seeds. Chop the tomato flesh into large chunks.

2 Heat the olive oil in a large saucepan. Add the onion, carrot and celery and cook over a medium-low heat for 3–4 minutes, stirring occasionally.

3 Add the tomatoes and their juice, with the garlic and marjoram. Cook for 2 minutes.

Stir in the water, reduce the heat and simmer, covered, for about 45 minutes until the vegetables are very soft, stirring occasionally.

4 Allow the soup to cool slightly, then transfer to a blender or food processor and purée until smooth, working in batches, if necessary. (If using a food processor, strain off the cooking liquid and reserve. Purée the soup solids with enough cooking liquid to moisten them, then combine with the remaining liquid.)

5 Return the soup to the saucepan and place over a medium-low heat. Add the cream and stir in the basil. Season with salt and pepper and heat through; do not allow to boil.

6 Ladle the soup into warm bowls and swirl a little extra cream into each serving. Serve at once.

COOK'S TIP

For the best flavour, this soup needs to be made with ripe tomatoes. If supermarket tomatoes are pale and hard, leave them to ripen at room temperature for several days. This is especially important in winter when most tomatoes are picked and shipped before they are ripe.

Spinach Soup

This soup has a rich brilliant colour and an intense pure flavour. You can taste the goodness!
Ready-washed spinach makes it especially quick to make.

Serves 4

INGREDIENTS

1 tbsp olive oil
1 onion, halved and thinly sliced
1 leek, split lengthways and thinly sliced
1 potato, finely diced

1 litre/1¾ pints/4 cups water
2 sprigs fresh marjoram or ¼ tsp dried
2 sprigs fresh thyme or ¼ tsp dried
1 bay leaf
400 g/14 oz young spinach, washed

freshly grated nutmeg
salt and pepper
4 tbsp single (light) cream, to serve

1 Heat the oil in a heavy-based saucepan over a medium heat. Add the onion and leek and cook for about 3 minutes, stirring occasionally, until they begin to soften.

2 Add the potato, water, marjoram, thyme and bay leaf, along with a large pinch of salt. Bring to the boil, reduce the heat, cover and cook gently for about 25 minutes until the vegetables are tender. Remove the bay leaf and the herb stems.

3 Add the spinach and continue cooking for 3–4 minutes, stirring frequently, just until it is completely wilted.

4 Allow the soup to cool slightly, then transfer to a blender or food processor and purée until smooth, working in batches if necessary. (If using a food processor, strain off the cooking liquid and reserve. Purée the soup solids with enough cooking liquid to moisten them, then combine with the remaining liquid.)

5 Return the soup to the saucepan and thin with a little more water, if wished. Season with salt, a good grinding of pepper and a generous grating of nutmeg. Place over a low heat and simmer until reheated.

6 Ladle the soup into warm bowls and swirl a table-spoonful of cream into each serving.

Roasted Pumpkin & Tomato Soup

This soup is a wonderful way to use autumn harvest vegetables. Make it when tomatoes are still plentiful and pumpkins are appearing in the farm markets.

Serves 4

INGREDIENTS

1–2 tbsp olive oil
900 g/2 lb peeled pumpkin flesh, cut into slices 2 cm/¾ inch thick
450 g/1 lb ripe tomatoes, skinned, cored and thickly sliced
1 onion, chopped

2 garlic cloves, finely chopped
4 tbsp white wine
2 tbsp water
600 ml/1 pint/2½ cups chicken or vegetable stock

120 ml/4 fl oz/½ cup single (light) cream
salt and pepper
snipped chives, to garnish

1 Drizzle 1 tablespoon of the olive oil over the base of a large baking dish. Layer the pumpkin, tomatoes, onion and garlic in 2 or 3 layers. Drizzle the top with the remaining olive oil, pour over the wine and water. Season with a little salt and pepper.

2 Cover with kitchen foil and bake in a preheated oven at 190°C/375°F/Gas Mark 5 for about 45 minutes, or until all the vegetables are soft.

3 Allow the vegetables to cool slightly, then transfer to a blender or food processor and add the cooking juices and as much stock as needed to cover the vegetables. Purée until smooth, working in batches if necessary.

4 Pour the purée into a saucepan and stir in the remaining stock. Cook gently over a medium heat, stirring occasionally, for about 15 minutes, or until heated through. Stir in the cream and continue cooking for 3–4 minutes.

5 Taste and adjust the seasoning, if necessary. Ladle the soup into warm bowls, garnish with chives and serve.

VARIATIONS

Serve the soup with crispy garlic croûtons, if you wish, instead of chives. You could substitute butternut or acorn squash for the pumpkin.

Celery & Stilton Soup

This soup combines two ingredients that have been paired since Victorian times, when celery stalks were put in tall glass containers on the dining table, to eat with Stilton cheese.

Serves 4

INGREDIENTS

2 tbsp butter
1 onion, finely chopped
4 large stalks celery, peeled and
  finely chopped
1 large carrot, finely chopped

1 litre/1¾ pints/4 cups chicken or
  vegetable stock
3–4 thyme sprigs
1 bay leaf

120 ml/4 fl oz/½ cup double (heavy)
  cream
150 g/5 ½ oz Stilton cheese, crumbled
freshly grated nutmeg
salt and pepper

---

1 Melt the butter in a large saucepan over a medium-low heat. Add the onion and cook for 3–4 minutes, stirring frequently, until just softened. Add the celery and carrot and continue cooking for 3 minutes. Season lightly with salt and pepper.

2 Add the stock, thyme and bay leaf and bring to the boil. Reduce the heat, cover and simmer gently for about 25 minutes, stirring occasionally, until the vegetables are very tender.

3 Allow the soup to cool slightly and remove the bouquet garni. Transfer the soup to a blender or food processor and purée until smooth, working in batches, if necessary. (If using a food processor, strain off the cooking liquid and reserve. Purée the soup solids with enough cooking liquid to moisten them, then combine with the remaining liquid.)

4 Return the puréed soup to the saucepan and stir in the cream. Simmer over a low heat for 5 minutes.

5 Add the Stilton slowly, stirring constantly, until smooth. (Do not allow the soup to boil.) Taste and adjust the seasoning, adding salt, if needed, plenty of pepper and nutmeg to taste.

6 Ladle into warm bowls, garnish with celery leaves and serve.

VARIATION

Substitute matured Cheddar or Gruyére for the Stilton.

Celeriac, Leek & Potato Soup

*It is hard to imagine that celeriac, a coarse, knobbly vegetable,
can taste so sweet. It makes a wonderfully flavourful soup.*

Serves 4

INGREDIENTS

1 tbsp butter
1 onion, chopped
2 large leeks, halved lengthways and
  sliced

1 large celeriac (about 750 g/
  1 lb 10 oz), peeled and cubed
1 potato, cubed
1 carrot, quartered and thinly sliced
1.2 litres/2 pints/5 cups water

⅛ tsp dried marjoram
1 bay leaf
freshly grated nutmeg
salt and pepper
celery leaves, to garnish

1 Melt the butter in a large
saucepan over a medium-low
heat. Add the onion and leeks and
cook for about 4 minutes, stirring
frequently, until just softened; do
not allow to colour.

2 Add the celeriac, potato,
carrot, water, marjoram and
bay leaf, with a large pinch of salt.
Bring to the boil, reduce the heat,
cover and simmer for about 25
minutes until the vegetables are
tender. Remove the bay leaf.

3 Allow the soup to cool
slightly. Transfer to a blender
or food processor and purée until
smooth. (If using food processor,
strain off cooking liquid and
reserve. Purée the soup solids with
enough cooking liquid to moisten
them, then combine with
remaining liquid.)

4 Return the puréed soup to
the saucepan and stir to
blend. Season with salt, pepper
and nutmeg. Simmer over a
medium-low heat until reheated.

5 Ladle the soup into warm
bowls, garnish with celery
leaves and serve.

Tarragon Pea Soup

This soup is simple and quick to make using frozen peas and stock made from a cube, ingredients you are likely to have on hand.

Serves 4

2 tsp butter
1 onion, finely chopped
2 leeks, finely chopped
1 ½ tbsp white rice

500 g/1 lb 2 oz frozen peas
1 litre/1¾ pints/4 cups water
1 chicken or vegetable stock cube
½ tsp dried tarragon

salt and pepper
chopped hard-boiled (hard-cooked)
   egg or croûtons, to garnish

1 Melt the butter in a large saucepan over a medium-low heat. Add the onion, leeks and rice. Cover and cook for about 10 minutes, stirring occasionally, until the vegetables are soft.

2 Add the peas, water, stock cube and tarragon and bring just to the boil. Season with a little pepper. Cover and simmer for about 35 minutes, stirring occasionally, until the vegetables are very tender.

3 Allow the soup to cool slightly, then transfer to a blender or food processor and purée until smooth, working in batches if necessary. (If using a food processor, strain off the cooking liquid and reserve. Purée the soup solids with enough cooking liquid to moisten them, then combine with the remaining liquid.)

4 Return the puréed soup to the saucepan. Taste and adjust the seasoning, adding plenty of pepper and, if needed, salt. Gently reheat the soup over a low heat for about 10 minutes until hot.

5 Ladle into warm bowls and garnish with egg or croûtons.

COOK'S TIP

The rice gives the soup a little extra body, but a small amount of raw or cooked potato would do the same job.

VARIATION

Substitute frozen green beans for the peas and omit the tarragon, replacing it with a little dried thyme and/or marjoram.

Roasted Garlic & Potato Soup

*The combination of potato, garlic and onion works brilliantly in soup.
In this recipe the garlic is roasted to give it added dimension and depth.*

Serves 4

INGREDIENTS

1 large bulb garlic with large cloves,
  peeled (about 100 g/3½ oz)
2 tsp olive oil
2 large leeks, thinly sliced
1 large onion, finely chopped
3 potatoes, diced (about 500 g/
  1 lb 2 oz)

1.2 litres/2 pints/5 cups chicken or
  vegetable stock
1 bay leaf
150 ml/5 fl oz/⅔ cup single (light)
  cream
freshly grated nutmeg
fresh lemon juice (optional)

salt and pepper
snipped fresh chives, to garnish

1 Put the garlic cloves in a baking dish, lightly brush with oil and bake in a preheated oven at 180°C/350°F/Gas Mark 4 for about 20 minutes until golden.

2 Heat the oil in a large saucepan over a medium heat. Add the leeks and onion, cover and cook for about 3 minutes, stirring frequently, until they begin to soften.

3 Add the potatoes, roasted garlic, stock and bay leaf.

Season with salt (unless the stock is salty) and pepper. Bring to the boil, reduce the heat, cover and cook gently for about 30 minutes until the vegetables are tender. Remove the bay leaf.

4 Allow the soup to cool slightly, then transfer to a blender or food processor and purée until smooth, working in batches if necessary. (If using a food processor, strain off the cooking liquid and reserve. Purée the soup solids with enough cooking liquid

to moisten them, then combine with the remaining liquid.)

5 Return the soup to the saucepan and stir in the cream and a generous grating of nutmeg. Taste and adjust the seasoning, if necessary, adding a few drops of lemon juice, if wished. Reheat over a low heat. Ladle into warm soup bowls, garnish with chives or parsley and serve.

Provençal Fish Soup

For the best results, you need to use flavourful fish, such as cod or haddock, for this recipe.
Frozen fish fillets are suitable, and there's no need to defrost them before cooking.

Serves 4–6

INGREDIENTS

1 tbsp olive oil
2 onions, finely chopped
1 small leek, thinly sliced
1 small carrot, finely chopped
1 stalk celery, finely chopped
1 small fennel bulb, finely chopped
  (optional)

3 garlic cloves, finely chopped
225 ml/8 fl oz/1 cup dry white wine
1.2 litres/2 pints/5 cups water
400 g/14 oz can tomatoes in juice
1 bay leaf
pinch of fennel seeds
2 strips orange rind

¼ tsp saffron threads
350 g/12 oz skinless white fish fillets
salt and pepper
garlic croûtons, to serve

1 Heat the oil in a large saucepan over a medium heat. Add the onions and cook for about 5 minutes, stirring frequently, until softened. Add the leek, carrot, celery, fennel and garlic and continue cooking for 4–5 minutes until the leek is wilted.

2 Add the wine and let it bubble for a minute. Add the tomatoes, bay leaf, fennel seeds, orange rind, saffron and water. Bring just to the boil, reduce the heat, cover and cook gently, stirring occasionally, for 30 minutes.

3 Add the fish and cook for a further 20–30 minutes until it is very soft and flaky. Remove the bay leaf and orange rind if possible.

4 Allow the soup to cool slightly, then transfer to a blender or food processor and purée until smooth, working in batches if necessary. (If using a food processor, strain off the cooking liquid and reserve. Purée the soup solids with enough cooking liquid to moisten them, then combine with the remaining liquid.)

5 Return the soup to the saucepan. Taste and adjust the seasoning, if necessary, and simmer for 5–10 minutes until heated through. Ladle the soup into warm bowls and sprinkle with croûtons.

Seafood Chowder

Mussels, an economical choice at the fishmonger, give essential flavour to this soup.
The proportions of fish and prawns (shrimp) are flexible – use more or less as you wish.

Serves 6

INGREDIENTS

1 kg/2 lb 4 oz mussels
4 tbsp plain (all-purpose) flour
1.5 litres/2¾ pints/6¼ cups fish stock
1 tbsp butter
1 large onion, finely chopped
350 g/12 oz skinless white fish fillets,

such as cod, sole or haddock
200 g/7 oz cooked or raw peeled
   prawns (shrimp)
300 ml/10 fl oz/1¼ cups whipping
   cream or double (heavy) cream

salt and pepper
snipped fresh dill, to garnish

1 Discard any broken mussels and those with open shells that do not close when tapped. Rinse, pull off any 'beards', and if there are barnacles, scrape them off with a knife under cold running water. Put the mussels in a large heavy-based saucepan. Cover tightly and cook over a high heat for about 4 minutes, or until the mussels open, shaking the pan occasionally. When they are cool enough to handle, remove the mussels from the shells, adding any additional juices to the cooking liquid. Strain the cooking liquid through a muslin-lined sieve and reserve.

2 Put the flour in a mixing bowl and very slowly whisk in enough of the stock to make a thick paste. Whisk in a little more stock to make a smooth liquid.

3 Melt the butter in heavy-based saucepan over a medium-low heat. Add the onion, cover and cook for about 5 minutes, stirring frequently, until it softens.

4 Add the remaining fish stock and bring to the boil. Slowly whisk in the flour mixture until well combined and bring back to the boil, whisking constantly. Add the mussel cooking liquid. Season with salt, if needed, and pepper. Reduce the heat and simmer, partially covered, for 15 minutes.

5 Add the fish and mussels and continue simmering, stirring occasionally, for about 5 minutes, or until the fish is cooked and begins to flake.

6 Stir in the prawns (shrimp) and cream. Taste and adjust the seasoning. Simmer for a few minutes longer to heat through. Ladle into warm bowls, sprinkle with dill and serve.

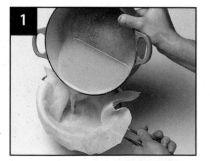

Crab Soup

This rich, tasty soup is simple to make and always popular. If you are feeling generous,
increase the amount of crab meat for a more luxurious soup.

Serves 4–6

INGREDIENTS

350 g/12 oz crab meat
4 tbsp butter
225 ml/8 fl oz/1 cup milk
1 large shallot, very finely chopped
4 tbsp plain (all purpose) flour

300 ml/10 fl oz/1¼ cups fish stock
300 ml/10 fl oz/1¼ cups whipping or
   double (heavy) cream
4 tbsp dry Oloroso sherry, or to taste

finely chopped fresh parsley, to
garnish

1 Pick over the crab meat to remove any bits of shell. Melt 1 tablespoon of the butter in a small saucepan over a very low heat. Add the crab meat, stir gently and add half the milk. Heat until bubbles appear around the edge and steam rises. Remove from the heat and set aside.

2 Melt the remaining butter in a large saucepan over a low heat. Add the shallot and cook gently for about 10 minutes until softened, stirring frequently; do not allow it to brown.

3 Stir in the flour and cook for 2 minutes. Whisk in the stock and remaining milk and bring to the boil, stirring constantly.

4 Gradually stir in the cream and season with salt and pepper to taste. Reduce the heat and simmer gently, stirring occasionally, for 10–15 minutes, until the shallots are soft and the soup is smooth and thick.

5 Stir in the crab meat mixture. If a thinner soup is preferred, add a little more stock or milk.

Stir in the sherry and simmer for about 5 minutes until heated through. Taste and adjust the seasoning, if necessary. Ladle the soup into warm bowls and garnish with parsley.

Vegetable Beef Soup

This soup is hearty and warming. It's a wonderful way to use fresh garden produce, but frozen vegetables are equally colourful and nutritious. No need to defrost them first.

Serves 6–8

INGREDIENTS

450 g/1 lb stewing steak
2 x 400 g/14 oz cans chopped
  tomatoes in juice
2 onions, finely chopped
2-3 garlic cloves, finely chopped
3 carrots, diced
2 stalks celery, sliced

150 g/5½ oz green cabbage, thinly
  sliced
1 bay leaf
5-6 allspice berries
¼ tsp dried thyme
¼ tsp dried marjoram
1 litre/1¾ pints/4 cups water

1 litre/1¾ pints/4 cups beef stock
200 g/7 oz green beans, cut into short
  pieces
150 g/5½ oz peas
150 g/5½ oz sweetcorn
salt and pepper

1 Trim all visible fat from the steak and cut into 1 cm/½ inch cubes. Put in a large saucepan with the tomatoes, onions, garlic, carrots, celery, cabbage, bay leaf, allspice, thyme, marjoram and water.

2 Bring to the boil over a medium-high heat, skimming off any foam that rises to the surface. Stir in the stock, reduce the heat and regulate it so that the soup boils very gently.

Season with salt and pepper. Cook, partially covered, for 1 hour, stirring occasionally.

3 Add the green beans, peas and sweetcorn. Continue cooking for 1 hour longer, or until the meat and vegetables are very tender.

4 Taste and adjust the seasoning, adding salt and pepper as necessary. Ladle into warm bowls and serve.

COOK'S TIP

For quick beef stock, dilute 1 stock cube in 1 litre/1¾ pints/4 cups water, or use a can of beef consommé made up to that quantity with water. Alternatively, you can use all water and add 1 tsp salt.

Cream of Chicken & Asparagus

This delectable soup is best made with fairly large asparagus with long stems.
Short-stemmed asparagus will give less flavour to the creamy soup base.

Serves 4

INGREDIENTS

350 g/12 oz asparagus
2 tsp butter
1 onion, halved and sliced
1 leek, sliced
60 g/2 oz/4 tbsp white rice

1 litre/1 ¾ pints/4 cups chicken stock
1 bay leaf
150 ml/5 fl oz/⅔ cup double
   (heavy) cream

175 g/6 oz cooked chicken, cut into
   thin slices
salt and pepper

1 Remove and discard woody bases of the asparagus. Using a vegetable peeler, peel the asparagus stems. Cut off the tips and set aside. Chop the stems into small pieces.

2 Bring a small saucepan of salted water to the boil and drop in the asparagus tips. Cook for 1–2 minutes until bright green and barely tender. If they are large, slice in half lengthways. Reserve the asparagus tips.

3 Heat the butter in a large saucepan over a medium heat and add the onion and leek. Cover and cook for 3–4 minutes, stirring frequently, until the onion is soft.

4 Add the asparagus stems, rice, stock and bay leaf with a pinch of salt. Bring just to the boil, reduce the heat, cover and simmer for 30–35 minutes or until the rice and vegetables are very soft. Remove the bay leaf.

5 Allow the soup to cool slightly, then transfer to a blender or food processor and purée until smooth, working in batches if necessary. (If using a food processor, strain off the cooking liquid and reserve. Purée the soup solids with enough cooking liquid to moisten them, then combine with the remaining liquid.)

6 Return the soup to the saucepan and place over a medium-low heat. Stir in the chicken and reserved asparagus tips, then the cream. Taste and adjust the seasoning, adding salt, if needed, and pepper. Simmer for 5–10 minutes until heated through, stirring occasionally. Ladle the soup into warm bowls and serve.

Chicken, Leek & Celery Soup

*This gently flavoured pale green soup is well balanced and very satisfying.
It is suitable either for a starter or light lunch.*

Serves 3–4

INGREDIENTS

1 litre/1¾ pints/4 cups chicken stock
1 bay leaf
200 g/7 oz skinless boned chicken
   breast
4 tbsp plain (all-purpose) flour
2 tsp butter

1 small onion, finely chopped
3 large leeks, including green parts,
   thinly sliced
2 stalks celery, peeled and thinly
   sliced
2 tbsp double (heavy) cream

freshly grated nutmeg
salt and pepper
fresh coriander leaves (cilantro) or
   parsley, to garnish

1 Heat the stock in a small saucepan with the bay leaf until it is steaming. Add the chicken breast and simmer gently for 20 minutes, or until firm to the touch. Discard the bay leaf. Remove the chicken and, when cool enough to handle, cut into small cubes.

2 Put the flour in a bowl. Very slowly whisk in enough of the stock to make a smooth liquid, adding about half the chicken stock.

3 Heat the butter in a heavy-based saucepan over a medium-low heat. Add the onion, leeks and half of the celery. Cook for about 5 minutes, stirring frequently, until the leeks begin to soften.

4 Slowly pour in the flour and stock mixture and bring to the boil, stirring constantly. Stir in the remaining stock, with a large pinch of salt if it is unsalted. Reduce the heat, cover and cook gently for about 25 minutes until the vegetables are tender.

5 Allow the soup to cool slightly, then transfer to a blender or food processor and purée until smooth, working in batches, if necessary. (If using a food processor, strain off the cooking liquid and reserve for later. Purée the soup solids with enough cooking liquid to moisten them, then combine with the remaining liquid.)

6 Return the soup to the saucepan and stir in the cream and nutmeg. Season with salt, if needed, and pepper. Place over a medium-low heat. Add the chicken breast and remaining celery to the soup. Simmer for about 15 minutes, until the celery is just tender, stirring occasionally. Taste and adjust the seasoning, ladle into warm bowls and sprinkle with coriander (cilantro) or parsley.

Turkey Soup with Rice, Mushrooms & Sage

This is a warming wintery soup, substantial enough to serve as a main course, with lots of crusty bread.

Serves 4–5

INGREDIENTS

3 tbsp butter
1 onion, finely chopped
1 stalk celery, finely chopped
25 large fresh sage leaves, finely chopped

4 tbsp plain (all-purpose) flour
1.2 litres/2 pints/5 cups turkey or chicken stock
100 g/3½ oz/⅔ cup brown rice
250 g/9 oz mushrooms, sliced

200 g/7 oz cooked turkey
200 ml/7 fl oz/¾ cup double (heavy) cream
freshly grated Parmesan cheese, to serve

1 Melt half the butter in a large saucepan over a medium-low heat. Add the onion, celery and sage and cook for 3-4 minutes until the onion is softened, stirring frequently. Stir in the flour and continue cooking for 2 minutes.

2 Slowly add about one quarter of the stock and stir well, scraping the bottom of the pan to mix in the flour. Pour in the remaining stock, stirring to combine completely, and bring just to the boil.

3 Stir in the rice and season with salt and pepper. Reduce the heat and simmer gently, partially covered, for about 30 minutes until the rice is just tender, stirring occasionally.

4 Meanwhile, melt the remaining butter in a large frying pan (skillet) over a medium heat. Add the mushrooms and season with salt and pepper. Cook for about 8 minutes until they are golden brown, stirring occasionally at first, then more often after they start to colour. Add the mushrooms to the soup.

5 Add the turkey to the soup and stir in the cream. Continue simmering for about 10 minutes until heated through. Taste and adjust the seasoning, if necessary. Ladle into warm bowls and serve with Parmesan cheese.

Minestrone

This winter vegetable soup makes good use of seasonal vegetables. Vary them according to what is available, including swede and winter squash if you wish.

Serves 6–8

INGREDIENTS

1 tbsp olive oil
1 onion, finely chopped
1 leek, halved lengthways and thinly sliced
2 garlic cloves, finely chopped
400 g/14 oz can chopped tomatoes in juice
1 carrot, finely diced
1 small turnip, finely diced

1 small potato, finely diced
125 g/4½ oz peeled celeriac (celery root), finely diced
250 g/9 oz peeled pumpkin flesh, finely diced
700 ml/1¼ pints/3 cups water
1 litre/1¾ pints/4 cups chicken or vegetable stock

400 g/14 oz can cannellini or borlotti beans, drained and rinsed
100 g/3½ oz leafy cabbage, such as cavolo nero
80 g/3 oz small pasta shapes or broken spaghetti
salt and pepper
freshly grated Parmesan cheese, to serve

1 Heat the oil in a large saucepan over a medium heat. Add the onion, leek and garlic and cook for 3–4 minutes, stirring occasionally, until slightly softened.

2 Add the tomatoes, carrot, turnip, potato, celeriac (celery root), pumpkin, water and stock. Bring to the boil, stirring occasionally.

3 Stir in the beans and cabbage. Season lightly with salt and pepper. Reduce the heat and simmer, partially covered, for about 50 minutes until all the vegetables are tender.

4 Bring salted water to the boil in a saucepan. Add the pasta and cook until it is just tender. Drain and add to the soup.

5 Taste the soup and adjust the seasoning. Ladle into warm bowls and serve with Parmesan cheese to sprinkle on top.

COOK'S TIP

The dark leaves of the Italian cabbage, cavolo nero, are particularly attractive in this colourful soup.

Split Pea & Ham Soup

A hearty and heartwarming soup, this is perfect for weekend lunches – or make it ahead for a nourishing mid-week supper, all ready to reheat.

Serves 6–8

INGREDIENTS

500 g/1 lb 2 oz split green peas
1 tbsp olive oil
1 large onion, finely chopped
1 large carrot, finely chopped
1 stalk celery, finely chopped

1 litre/1¾ pints/4 cups chicken or
    vegetable stock
1 litre/1¼ pints/4 cups water
225 g/8 oz lean smoked ham, finely
    diced

¼ tsp dried thyme
¼ tsp dried marjoram
1 bay leaf
salt and pepper

1 Rinse the peas under cold running water. Put in a saucepan and cover generously with water. Bring to the boil and boil for 3 minutes, skimming off the foam from the surface. Drain the peas.

2 Heat the oil in a large saucepan over a medium heat. Add the onion and cook for 3–4 minutes, stirring occasionally, until just softened.

3 Add the carrot and celery and continue cooking for 2 minutes. Add the peas, pour over the stock and water and stir to combine.

4 Bring just to the boil and stir the ham into the soup. Add the thyme, marjoram and bay leaf. Reduce the heat, cover and cook gently for 1–1½ hours until the ingredients are very soft. Remove the bay leaf.

5 Taste and adjust the seasoning. Ladle into warm soup bowls and serve.

VARIATION

You could add sliced, cooked sausages instead of or in addition to the ham. If you have a ham bone, use in place of the diced ham. Trim off the fat and cook the bone in the soup. Before serving, remove the bone, cut off the meat and return the meat to the soup.

Spicy Potato & Chick-pea (Garbanzo Bean) Soup

This soup uses ingredients you are likely to have on hand, yet it is far from standard fare. Spicy and substantial, it makes a delicious meal-in-a-bowl, ideal for a mid-week supper.

Serves 4

INGREDIENTS

1 tbsp olive oil
1 large onion, finely chopped
2–3 garlic cloves, finely chopped or
   crushed
1 carrot, quartered and thinly sliced
250 g/12 oz potatoes, diced
¼ tsp ground turmeric
¼ tsp garam masala

¼ tsp mild curry powder
400 g/14 oz can chopped tomatoes
   in juice
850 ml/1½ pints/3¾ cups water
400 g/14 oz can chopped tomatoes
   in juice
¼ tsp chilli puree (paste), or
   to taste

400 g/14 oz can chick-peas (garbanzo
   beans), rinsed and drained
80 g/3 oz fresh or frozen peas
salt and pepper
chopped fresh coriander (cilantro), to
   garnish

1 Heat the olive oil in a large saucepan over a medium heat. Add the onion and garlic and cook for 3–4 minutes, stirring occasionally, until the onion is beginning to soften.

2 Add the carrot, potatoes, turmeric, garam masala and curry powder and continue cooking for 1–2 minutes.

3 Add the tomatoes, water, and chilli purée (paste) with a large pinch of salt. Reduce the heat, cover and simmer for 30 minutes, stirring occasionally.

4 Add the chick-peas (garbanzo beans) and peas to the pan, continue cooking for about 15 minutes, or until all the vegetables are tender.

5 Taste the soup and adjust the seasoning, if necessary, adding a little more chilli if wished. Ladle into warm soup bowls and sprinkle with coriander (cilantro).

Tomato & Lentil Soup

This soup is simple and satisfying, with subtle, slightly exotic flavours.
It uses ingredients you are likely to have on hand, so it's ideal for a last-minute meal.

Serves 6

INGREDIENTS

1 tbsp olive oil
1 leek, thinly sliced
1 large carrot, quartered and thinly
  sliced
1 large onion, finely chopped
2 garlic cloves, finely chopped

250 g/9 oz split red lentils
1.2 litres/2 pints/5 cups water
350 ml/12 fl oz/1½ cups tomato juice
400 g/14 oz can chopped tomatoes
  in juice
¼ tsp ground cumin

¼ tsp ground coriander
1 bay leaf
salt and pepper
chopped fresh dill or parsley,
  to garnish

1 Heat the oil in a large saucepan over a medium heat. Add the leek, carrot, onion and garlic. Cover and cook for 4–5 minutes, stirring frequently, until the leek and onion are slightly softened.

2 Rinse and drain the lentils (check for any small stones). Add the lentils to the pan and stir in the water, tomato juice and tomatoes. Add the cumin, coriander and bay leaf with a large pinch of salt. Bring to the boil, reduce the heat and simmer for about 45 minutes, or until the vegetables are tender.

3 If you prefer a smooth soup, allow it to cool slightly, then transfer to a blender or food processor and purée until smooth, working in batches if necessary. (If using a food processor, strain off the cooking liquid and reserve. Purée the soup solids with enough cooking liquid to moisten them, then combine with the remaining liquid.) Only purée about half of the soup, if you prefer a more chunky soup.

4 Return the puréed soup to the saucepan and stir to blend. Season with salt and pepper to taste. Simmer over a medium-low heat until reheated.

5 Ladle the soup into warm bowls, garnish with dill or parsley and serve.

Golden Vegetable Soup with Green Lentils

In this simple-to-make soup, the flavours meld after blending to create a delicious taste. It is also very healthy and looks appealing.

Serves 6

INGREDIENTS

1 tbsp olive oil
1 onion, finely chopped
1 garlic clove, finely chopped
1 carrot, halved and thinly sliced
450 g/1 lb young green cabbage, cored, quartered and thinly sliced

400 g/14 oz can chopped tomatoes in juice
½ tsp dried thyme
2 bay leaves
1.5 litres/2¾ pints/6¼ cups chicken or vegetable stock

200 g/7 oz Puy lentils
450 ml/16 fl oz/2 cups water
salt and pepper
fresh coriander leaves (cilantro) or parsley, to garnish

1 Heat the oil in a large saucepan over a medium heat, add the onion, garlic and carrot and cook for 3–4 minutes, stirring frequently, until the onion starts to soften. Add the cabbage and cook for a further 2 minutes.

2 Add the tomatoes, thyme and 1 bay leaf, then pour in the stock. Bring to the boil, reduce the heat to low and cook gently, partially covered, for about 45 minutes until the vegetables are tender.

3 Meanwhile, put the lentils in another saucepan with the remaining bay leaf and the water. Bring just to the boil, reduce the heat and simmer for about 25 minutes until tender. Drain off any remaining water, and set aside.

4 When the vegetable soup is cooked, allow it to cool slightly, then transfer to a blender or food processor and purée until smooth, working in batches, if necessary. (If using a food processor, strain off the cooking liquid and reserve. Purée the soup solids with enough cooking liquid to moisten them, then combine with the remaining liquid.)

5 Return the soup to the saucepan and add the cooked lentils. Taste and adjust the seasoning, and cook for about 10 minutes to heat through. Ladle into warm bowls and garnish with coriander leaves (cilantro) or parsley.

French Onion Soup

A rich, flavourful homemade stock is the key to this satisfying soup.
While beef stock is traditional, a rich, intense chicken stock would be delicious as well.

Serves 6

INGREDIENTS

1 tbsp butter
2 tbsp olive oil
1 kg/2 lb 4 oz large yellow onions,
   halved and sliced into half-circles

3 large garlic cloves, finely chopped
2 tbsp plain (all-purpose) flour
200 ml/7 fl oz/³⁄₄ cup dry white wine
2 litres/3½ pints/8 cups beef stock

3 tbsp Cognac or brandy
6 slices French bread
200 g/7 oz Gruyére cheese, grated
salt and pepper

1 Melt the butter with the oil in a large heavy-based saucepan over a medium heat. Add the onions and cook, covered, for 10–12 minutes until they soften, stirring occasionally. Add the garlic and sprinkle with salt and pepper.

2 Reduce the heat a little and continue cooking, uncovered, for 30–35 minutes, or until the onions turn a deep, golden brown, stirring from time to time until they start to colour, then stirring more frequently and scraping the bottom of the pan as they begin to stick (see Cook's Tip).

3 Sprinkle over the flour and stir to blend. Stir in the white wine and bubble for 1 minute. Pour in the stock and bring to the boil, scraping the bottom of the pan and stirring to combine well. Reduce the heat to low, add the Cognac or brandy and simmer gently, stirring occasionally, for 45 minutes.

4 Toast the bread under a preheated hot grill (broiler) on one side. Turn over and top with the cheese, dividing it evenly. Grill (broil) until the cheese melts.

5 Place a piece of cheese toast in each of the 6 warmed bowls, then ladle the hot soup over. Serve at once.

COOK'S TIP

Don't try to hurry this soup. The rich flavour comes from cooking the onions slowly so their natural sugar caramelizes, then brewing them with the stock.

Watercress Vichyssoise

Traditional vichyssoise is simply cold leek and potato soup flavoured with chives.
The addition of watercress gives it a refreshing flavour and lovely cool colour.

Serves 6

INGREDIENTS

1 tbsp olive oil
3 large leeks, thinly sliced (about
   350 g/12 oz)
1 large potato, finely diced (about
   350 g/12 oz)

600 ml/1 pint/2½ cups chicken or
   vegetable stock
450 ml/16 fl oz/2 cups water
1 bay leaf
175 g/6 oz prepared watercress

200 ml/7 fl oz/¾ cup single (light)
   cream
salt and pepper
watercress leaves, to garnish

1 Heat the oil in a heavy-based saucepan over a medium heat. Add the leeks and cook for about 3 minutes, stirring frequently, until they begin to soften.

2 Add the potato, stock, water and bay leaf. Add salt if the stock is unsalted. Bring to the boil, reduce the heat, cover and cook gently for about 25 minutes until the vegetables are tender. It may be difficult to find the bay leaf, however it is best removed.

3 Add the watercress and continue to cook for a further 2–3 minutes, stirring frequently, just until the watercress is completely wilted.

4 Allow the soup to cool slightly, then transfer to a blender or food processor and purée until smooth, working in batches if necessary. (If using a food processor, strain off the cooking liquid and reserve. Purée the soup solids with enough cooking liquid to moisten them, then combine with the remaining liquid.)

5 Put the soup in a large bowl and stir in half the cream. Season with salt, if needed, and plenty of pepper.

6 Refrigerate until cold. Taste and adjust the seasoning, if necessary. Ladle into chilled bowls, drizzle the remaining cream on top and garnish with watercress leaves. Serve at once.

This is a Parragon Publishing Book
This edition published in 2007

Parragon Publishing
Queen Street House
4 Queen Street, Bath, BA1 1HE, UK

Copyright © Parragon 2003

All recipes and photography compiled from material
created by 'Haldane Mason', and 'The Foundry'.

Cover design by Shelley Doyle.

ISBN: 978-1-4075-1099-6

Printed in Malaysia

NOTE

Cup measurements in this book are for American cups. This book uses
imperial and metric measurements. Follow the same units of measurement
throughout; do not mix imperial and metric. All spoon measurements are
level; teaspoons are assumed to be 5 ml and tablespoons are assumed to be
15 ml. Unless otherwise stated, milk is assumed to be whole milk, eggs
and individual vegetables such as potatoes are medium, and pepper is
freshly ground black pepper.

The times given for each recipe are an approximate guide only because
the preparation times may differ according to the techniques used by
different people and the cooking times may vary as a result of the
type of oven used.

Recipes using raw or very lightly cooked eggs should be avoided by
infants, the elderly, pregnant women, convalescents and anyone
suffering from an illness.